FROM DANNY BOY TO BLACK HOLE SUN

10 Jazz Arrangements for Solo Piano

by John Colianni

Cover Photo by James Gudeman

“HIS NIMBLE FINGERS MOVE WITH THE GRACE OF ART TATUM AND THE SPEED OF OSCAR PETERSON.”

—Down Beat Magazine

“JOHN COLIANNI IS THE ESSENCE OF A SWING PIANIST, MUCH AS EARL HINES WAS . . . GIVING EVERYTHING A STRONG, SWINGING PULSE.”

—*John S. Wilson,* New York Times

“THE BEST PIANIST I HAVE EVER WORKED WITH.”

—*Mel Tormé*

“JOHN IS DESTINED FOR GREATNESS.”

—*Milt Hinton*

Concord Records

MEET JOHN

John Colianni has built his reputation as a talented young pianist who has embraced and mastered jazz's pre-bebop–era styles and mindset. An artist whose musical style pays homage to such piano greats as Teddy Wilson, Art Tatum and Oscar Peterson, John imparts his swinging, yet unique, melodic touch and blistering virtuosity to a strikingly diverse collection of tunes—from swing-era Tatum to grunge-rock pioneers Nirvana. "I prefer swing jazz, music that incorporates pop tunes, musical theatre, and classical music that offers a greater means of expression," John says. "Actually, I like music for its own sake, which to me usually means swing."

John was born in Paterson, New Jersey, on January 7, 1963. His parents were an important influence in the development of his early musical tastes. He frequently played their Jimmie Lunceford, Duke Ellington and Count Basie records, and would often go to bed with headphones on listening to the artistry of Tatum, Wilson and Peterson. His only formal training consisted of four years of tutelage with Washington, D.C., pianist Lester Kerr, a longtime colleague and student of the great swing pianist Wilson. As an adolescent, John often sat in at jazz clubs with the likes of Clark Terry, Roy Eldridge, Maxine Sullivan and Anita O'Day. His professional debut occurred at D.C.'s legendary jazz club Blues Alley. He was all of 15 years old.

At age 18 John mustered up enough courage to sneak backstage at a $300-per-plate New Year's Eve bash in an Atlantic City casino. He found orchestra leader and vibraphone legend Lionel Hampton conversing in a hallway and introduced himself. "Mr. Hampton," he said, "my name's John, and I play piano." An orchestra member passing by called out, "He plays a damn good piano!" Hamp's immediate response was to arrange an audition in his New York City apartment the next morning. That evening, John was jet-bound to California to perform his first gig with the Lionel Hampton All-Stars.

After two years with the Lionel Hampton organization, John began touring with his own trio, quartet and big band, appearing in major jazz venues in the U.S., Canada, and all across Europe. Along the way, he garnered the $3,000 prize in the International Thelonious Monk Competition (Smithsonian Institution, Washington, D.C.).

John is a great favorite of the owner of Michael's Pub in Manhattan, where Mel Tormé was performing an extended engagement in 1990. Upon hearing John's CD's being played during one of Tormé's set breaks, Mel was so enthralled that he immediately demanded John's phone number. The next morning Tormé phoned John at his home in New Jersey, informing him he was hired and that he was to be flown to gigs in Phoenix the following week. In Phoenix, John learned that Mel's bass player's instrument had been destroyed in transit—John would play his debut performance with Tormé simultaneously sight-reading the piano arrangements and playing the bass parts with his left hand. Four fruitful years as Tormé's musical director/pianist followed.

With Hamp and Tormé, John has made 29 appearances with major symphonies in the U.S. and Canada. He has appeared on 10 recordings for Concord Jazz—three of his own, the rest with Hamp and Tormé—and has gigged as bandleader and soloist in venues from Los Angeles to Switzerland. *And* he is authoring a series of articles on piano accompaniment for vocalists. Pretty heady stuff for a man barely into his 30s!

Of his own repertoire John says, "I look for songs that have a couple of elements: a memorable melody that haunts, that has some emotion, that engages a response beyond the intellectual. And rhythmically I enjoy things that swing."

NOTES FROM JOHN

This book consists of annotated interpretations of jazz and jazz-oriented themes covering a wide variety of styles and periods—from traditional folk ("Danny Boy") to contemporary hard rock (Soundgarden's "Black Hole Sun"). In presenting these selections, this book is not conceived as an instructional study; rather, I hope to give you, the player, a sampling of how flexible and dynamic jazz piano can be. Along the way, you'll also learn about specific jazz piano techniques.

Some styles of jazz, such as stride and ragtime, demand a good deal of digital dexterity. Blues and funk are more effectively rendered with a cruder, more visceral approach. An engaging mix of "clean" and "funky" techniques can be heard in the course of one jazz solo. In jazz, good technique can be a tremendous asset and should certainly be realized to the highest degree attainable, but technique is not everything. Keep this in mind if you find that your technique is not quite up to one or two of the trickier passages encountered in this book.

The technically easier pieces are as musically rewarding to the composer as any of the more advanced pieces. In the beginning, stick to the selections with which you are comfortable. Much of the special feeling in a good jazz performance depends upon the degree to which the player can relax and "get in the groove." You may be surprised to learn that by assimilating this concept into a regular routine, your jazz piano technique will advance significantly.

I hope you enjoy playing these pieces as much as I have enjoyed arranging and writing them for you.

John Colianni
September 1995

CONTENTS

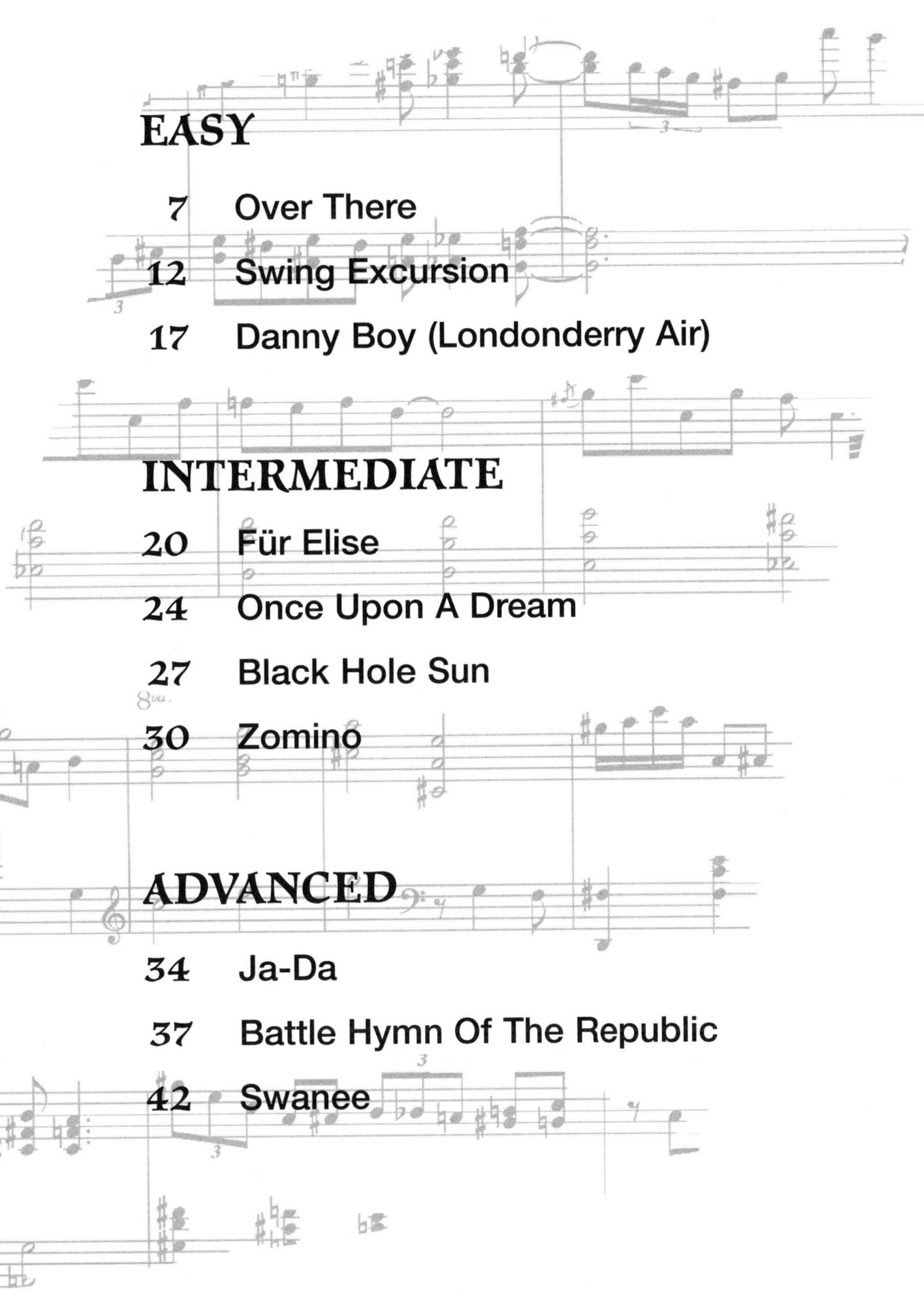

EASY

INTERMEDIATE

ADVANCED

PERFORMANCE NOTES

EASY

OVER THERE

This song dates back to World War I. It was originally conceived as a quick march, but the melody adapts well to the medium lope (or *tempo*) called for here. The grace noted chord 2 1/2 beats into the last measure is easily played by sliding from D♯ to E with the 2nd finger. This method is very effective for achieving a "funky, bluesy" sound.

SWING EXCURSION

This is an original based loosely on the harmonic pattern of Gershwin's "I Got Rhythm." In fact, there are numerous pieces based on this all-time classic song.

The chord foundation of "I Got Rhythm," which makes use of a I, mVI7, mII, V7 harmonic pattern, offers innumerable opportunities for improvisation. In terms of chord symbols, this pattern, in the key of B♭, would read: B♭, Gm7, Cm, F7—with each chord two beats in duration. "Swing Excursion," like "I Got Rhythm," is 32 bars in length and is divided into four sections—AABA structure—wherein section "B," bars 17-24, constitutes the *release* (or *bridge*) of the song. The melody and harmony in the "B" section of the song are meant to stand apart from the "A" sections, which consist largely of one recurring, 8-bar theme. This arrangement offers some of the possibilities for extemporaneous development of a theme, which has become universal in jazz music.

DANNY BOY (LONDONDERRY AIR)

Jazz is a terrific medium for combining two or more distinct styles of music. In this case, a haunting melody from long-ago Ireland is flavored along its way with a few open-position jazz chord voicings. This arrangement is good practice for rhythmically free playing. Try to bring the piece's heavily emotional import to the fore in your interpretation.

INTERMEDIATE

FÜR ELISE

This is a good example of a transformation of meter. "Für Elise" was written by Beethoven in 3/4. Here, we are "swinging it" in 4/4. So that the desired contrast with the original can be realized, play with a sharp attack throughout the first eight bars of the melody. The bluesy figures in the coda are the easiest and are most effectively played by exaggerating the arch of the hand and fingers, and by the turning of the wrists from left to right. (Roll over, Beethoven.)

ONCE UPON A DREAM

Songs from contemporary musicals tend to be overlooked by jazz performers, often undeservedly so. This song is from the popular stage musical *Jekyll & Hyde*. Some players with smaller hands may find some of the left-hand stretches somewhat challenging. If you are unable to span a stretch, simply roll it, from the bottom up, with a little pedalling to glue the chord together.

You can increase your span, to a degree, through practice. Whatever exercises you use to increase your stretch will be more beneficial if your hand is as relaxed and supple as possible—maintaining just enough firmness to play the notes cleanly and accurately.

BLACK HOLE SUN

A solo piano rendition of a "grunge" rock tune will sink or swim based on the pianist's attitude toward the piece. A jazz performer should play a piece like this with the same passion and conviction he or she brings to more conventionally played songs. For some, this may mean abandoning a negative disposition toward a song by virtue of its origin or genre (i.e. "rock 'n' roll" or "pop").

Anything worth doing is worth doing well, and this song *is* worth doing well. This piece should be played with a surging rhythmic impetus, employing straight, or even 8th notes only. Dynamics are very important here and should be well defined. The forte sections should be approached somewhat thunderously, with an equal degree of tenderness in the delicate portions.

ZOMINO

This is a medium tempo blues. In this arrangement, there is a good deal of simultaneous right hand/left hand independence. It's always good practice to do both hands separately first before attempting to play the piece using both hands together.

ADVANCED

JA-DA

If you are unaccustomed to playing in the stride style, you will find this solo to be a good workout for your left hand. Full, two-handed piano is not as common today as it was in the earlier periods of jazz. Again, for some of the more difficult left-hand spans, rolling the chords is recommended.

BATTLE HYMN OF THE REPUBLIC

Special attention should again be given to the left hand. Also try to infuse your playing with a "gospel" spirit, which is implied at several points throughout the piece. The choppy treble figures, accompanied by the descending, broken, left-hand 10th chords, may remind some of Gershwin's brilliant piano playing.

SWANEE

"Swanee" was composed in 1919. The big *tour-de-force* "Broadway" ending seems to be a good finale for this book. For the rapid passages, remember that accuracy and velocity are best maintained with a light, yet firm touch.

Over There

Words and Music by George M. Cohan

3
3

3
3
5
8vb

Swing Excursion

Music by John Colianni

Ped.

Ped.

3
3
3
Ped.

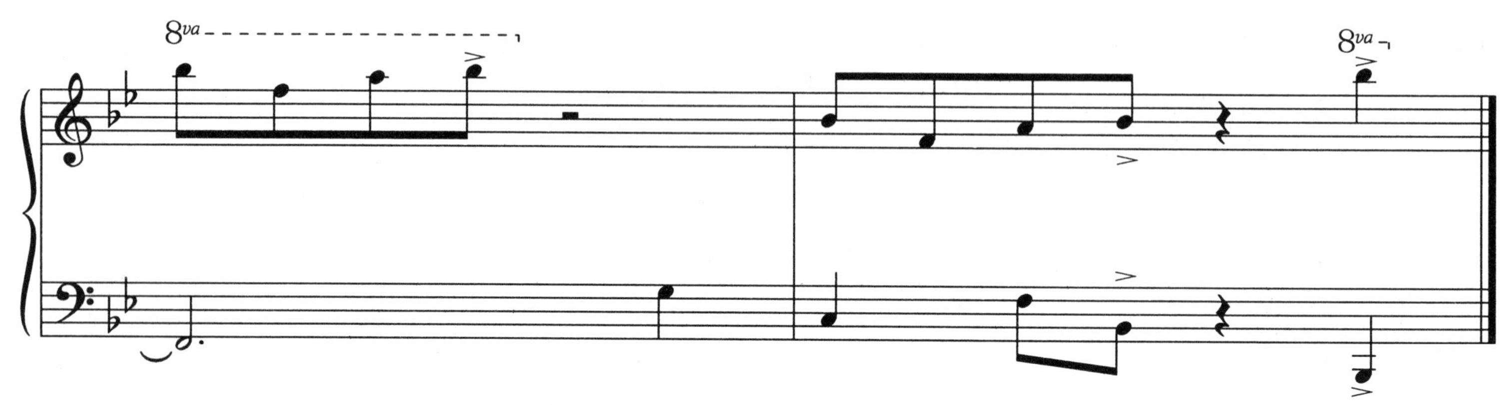
8va
8va

DANNY BOY (LONDONDERRY AIR)

Traditional

Ped.

3
Ped.
Ped.

f
Ped.

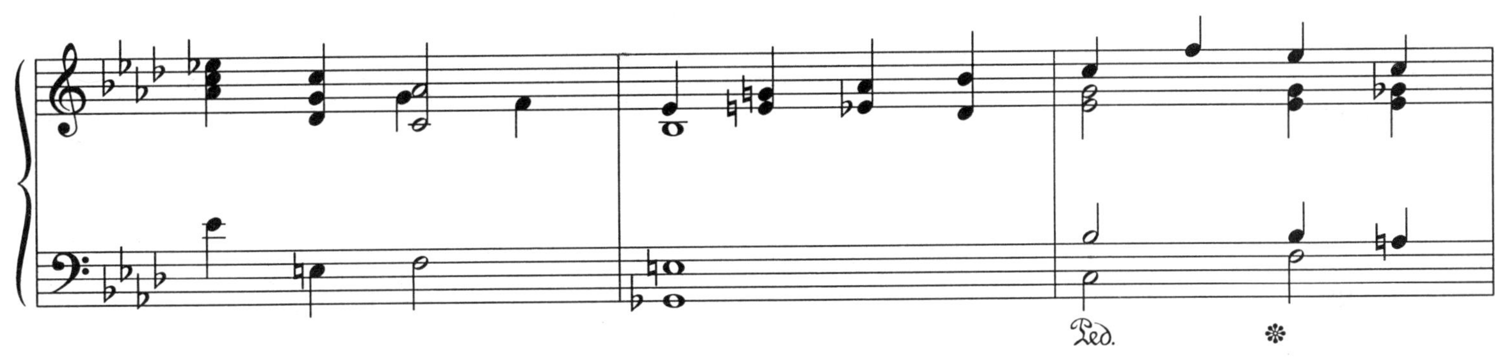
Ped.

To Coda
D.S. al Coda

Coda
Ped.

Für Elise

Music by Ludwig van Beethoven

8va
(8va)
To Coda

3
D.S. al Coda

Outbooks, Inc.
PO Box 536
Tontitown, AR 72770
UNITED STATES
support@onceuponatimebooks.com

Outbooks, Inc.
PO Box 536
Tontitown, AR 72770
UNITED STATES

To: Alibris APEX DC 76524176-80 - APEX
800 Avondale Ave.

Grandview Heights, OH 43212-3473
UNITED STATES

If this order is shipping from the US to an international buyer, remember to attach proper documentation. Complete and attach USPS Form CN-22 for all Priority Mail International Envelopes or First-Class Mail International shipments (available at your post office).

Order Number: 4609871
Ship Method: Standard
Customer Name: Alibris APEX DC 76524176-80 - APEX
Order Date: 7/6/2026
Alibris Order #: 76524176-80
Email:

Items:

Qty	Item	Locator	Item ID	Condition
1	From Danny Boy to Black Hole Sun: 10 Jazz Arrangements for Solo Piano John Colianni SKU: mon0003325154 ISBN: 0895249944 - Books	0003326374	76524176-80	Good

Notes:

This is a used book in good condition and may show some signs of use or wear. This is a used book in good condition and may show some signs of use or wear. paperback

alibris

Alibris guarantees the condition of every item as it is described on our Web site. If you are dissatisfied for any reason, return your purchase within 60 days of receipt for a refund of the item price. We'll also refund shipping costs if the return was a result of our error. All return requests must be submitted via the Alibris Web site. Any item returned without accompanying paperwork and/or more than 60 days after its shipment date will be discarded and you will not be eligible to receive a refund.

If you have any questions or concerns regarding this order, please contact us at support@onceuponatimebooks.com
Thanks for your order!

Coda

even ♪'s

p

Once Upon A Dream

Words by Leslie Bricusse
Music by Frank Wildhorn

*Even eighth notes, "pop" style

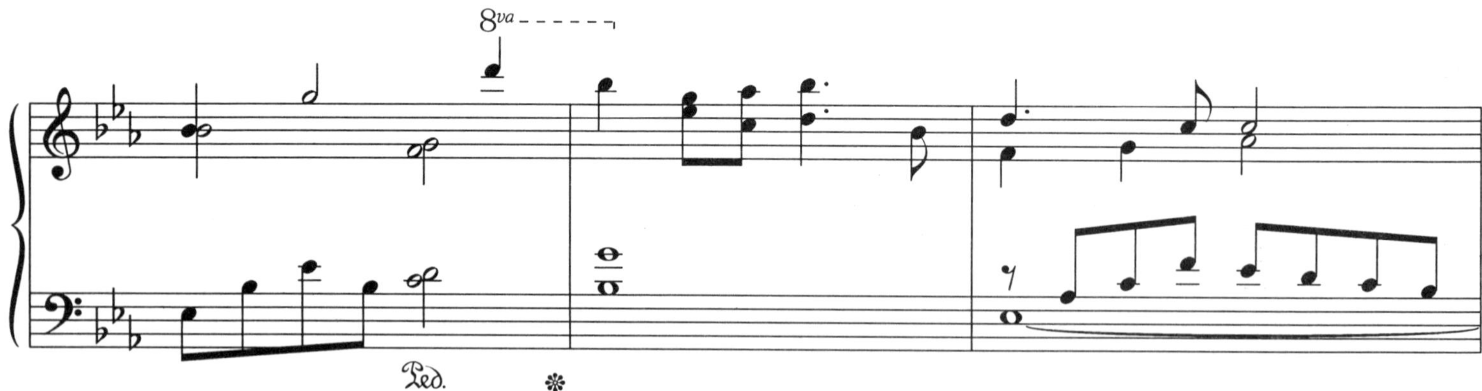

8va
8va
rit.
p
f
rapidly
5
loco
mp

Black Hole Sun

Words and Music by Chris Cornell

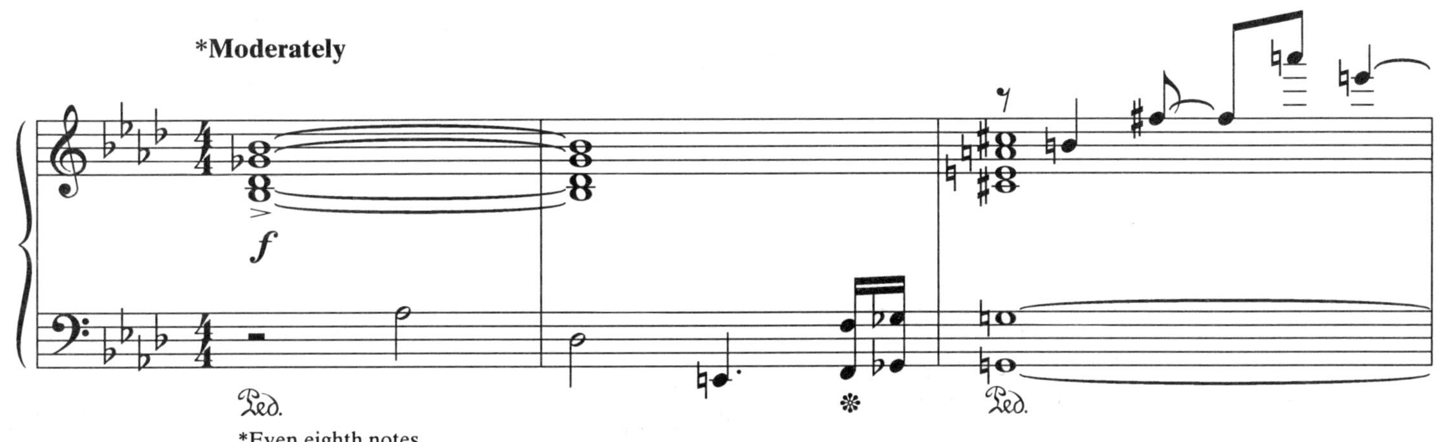

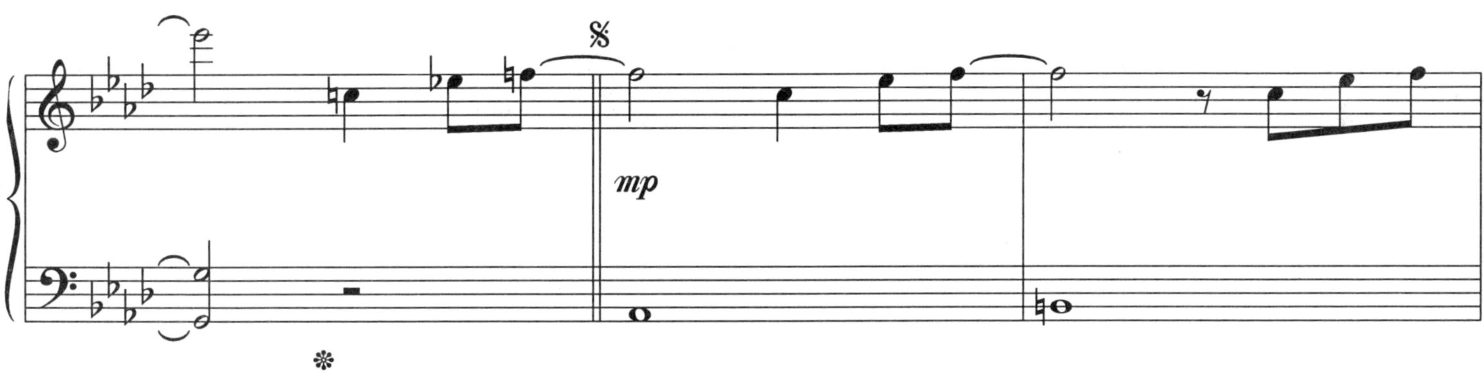

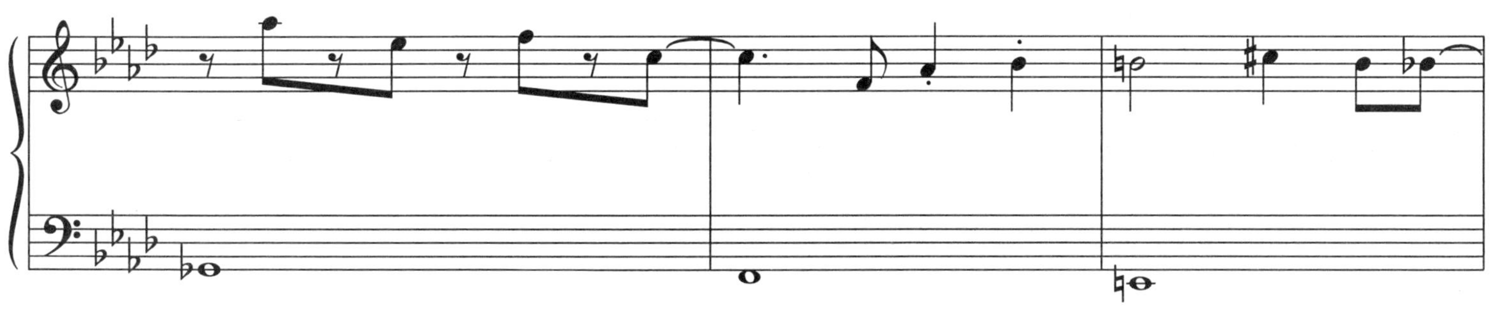

mf
Ped.
8va
To Coda

D.S. al Coda
Coda
f
ff
fff
L.H.
Ped.
Ped.

Zomino

Music by John Colianni

3
3
3
3
3

8va

Ja-Da

Music by B. Carelton

8va
8va

rit.
freely
slower
a tempo

BATTLE HYMN OF THE REPUBLIC

Traditional

8va
15
f
10
3
Moderate Swing
mf
3

f
mp
p

f

8va
loco
3
8va

Swanee

Words by Irving Caesar
Music by George Gershwin

Brightly

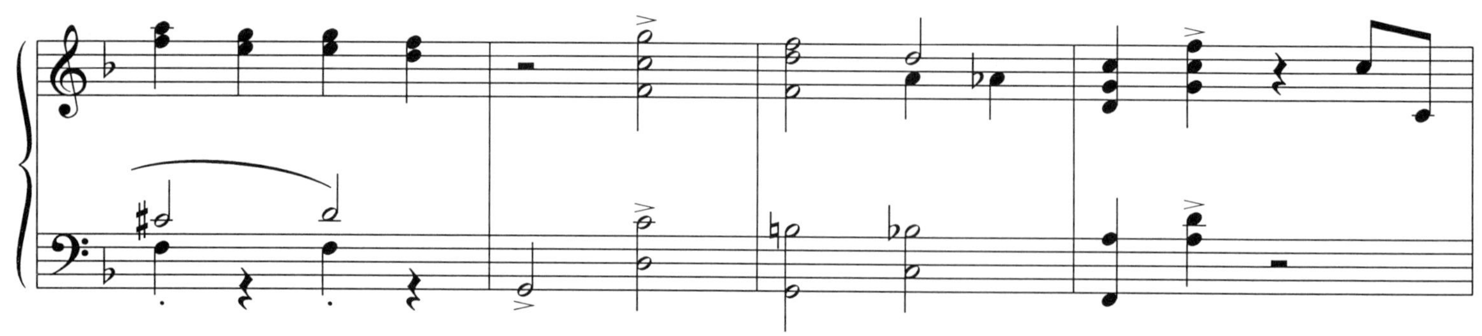

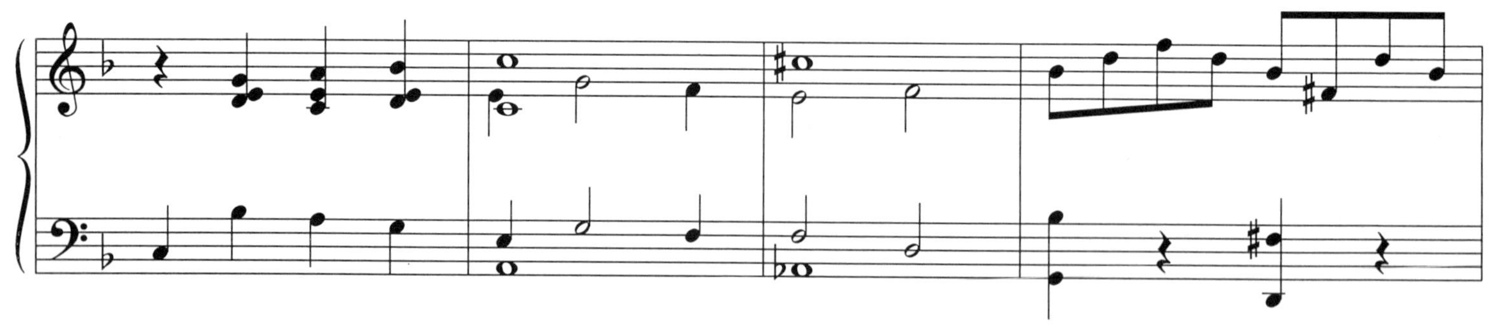

3

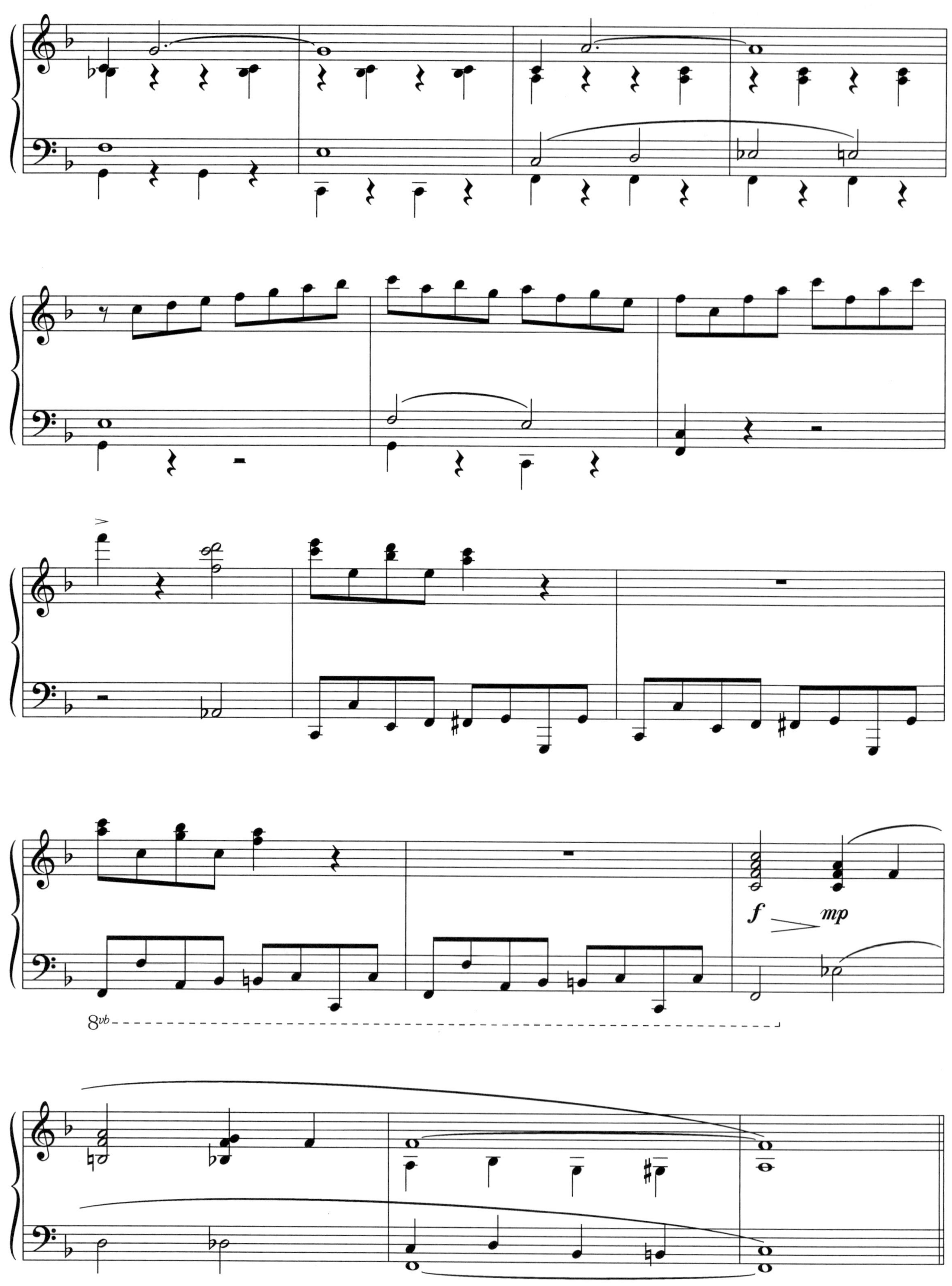

8vb
f
mp

Grandioso, freely
8va
rit.
15